133

THE

GOLDEN TREASURY
OF THE BEST SONGS AND LYRICAL
POEMS IN THE ENGLISH LANGUAGE

Oxford University Press, Amen House, London E.C. 4

EDINBURGH GLASGOW NEW YORK TORONTO MELBOURNE
WELLINGTON BOMBAY CALCUTTA MADRAS CAPE TOWN

Geoffrey Cumberlege, Publisher to the University

THE
GOLDEN TREASURY
OF THE BEST SONGS AND LYRICAL
POEMS IN THE ENGLISH LANGUAGE

Selected and arranged by
FRANCIS TURNER PALGRAVE

With Additional Poems

The World's Classics

Geoffrey Cumberlege
OXFORD UNIVERSITY PRESS
London   New York   Toronto

FRANCIS TURNER PALGRAVE

Born, Great Yarmouth, 28 September 1824
Died, South Kensington, 24 October 1897

The Golden Treasury of the best Songs and Lyrical Poems in the English language *was first published in* 1861. *In* The World's Classics *it was first published, with additional Poems, in* 1907, *and reprinted in* 1908, 1909, 1910, 1911, 1912, *and* 1913. *New edition,* 1914, *reprinted* 1914, 1916 *(twice),* 1917 *(twice),* 1918 *(thrice),* 1919 *(twice),* 1920 *(twice),* 1921, 1922, 1923, 1924, 1925, 1926. *A new edition with poems by contemporary writers was published in* 1928 *and reprinted in* 1928, 1929, 1930, 1931, 1933, 1935, 1936, 1938, *and (with further additional poems bringing the book up to date of publication) in* 1941. *Reprinted* 1943, 1944, 1947, *and* 1948.

PRINTED IN GREAT BRITAIN

CONTENTS

Εἰς τὸν λειμῶνα καθίσας,
ἔδρεπεν ἕτερον ἐφ' ἑτέρῳ
αἰρόμενος ἄγρευμ' ἀνθέων
ἁδομένᾳ ψυχᾷ.

[Eurip. *frag.* 754.]

[' He sat in the meadow and plucked
with glad heart the spoil of the
flowers, gathering them one by one.']

TO ALFRED TENNYSON

POET LAUREATE

THIS book in its progress has recalled often to my memory a man with whose friendship we were once honoured, to whom no region of English Literature was unfamiliar, and who, whilst rich in all the noble gifts of Nature, was most eminently distinguished by the noblest and the rarest,—just judgement and high-hearted patriotism. It would have been hence a peculiar pleasure and pride to dedicate what I have endeavoured to make a true national Anthology of three centuries to Henry Hallam. But he is beyond the reach of any human tokens of love and reverence ; and I desire therefore to place before it a name united with his by associations which, whilst Poetry retains her hold on the minds of Englishmen, are not likely to be forgotten.

Your encouragement, given while traversing the wild scenery of Treryn Dinas, led me to begin the work ; and it has been completed under your advice and assistance. For the favour now asked

I have thus a second reason : and to this I may add, the homage which is your right as Poet, and the gratitude due to a Friend, whose regard I rate at no common value.

Permit me then to inscribe to yourself a book which, I hope, may be found by many a lifelong fountain of innocent and exalted pleasure ; a source of animation to friends when they meet ; and able to sweeten solitude itself with best society, —with the companionship of the wise and the good, with the beauty which the eye cannot see, and the music only heard in silence. If this Collection proves a storehouse of delight to Labour and to Poverty,—if it teaches those indifferent to the Poets to love them, and those who love them to love them more, the aim and the desire entertained in framing it will be fully accomplished.

F. T. P.

May, 1861.

PREFACE

THIS little Collection differs, it is believed, from others in the attempt made to include in it all the best original Lyrical pieces and Songs in our language, by writers not living,—and none beside the best. Many familiar verses will hence be met with ; many also which should be familiar :—the Editor will regard as his fittest readers those who love Poetry so well, that he can offer them nothing not already known and valued.

The Editor is acquainted with no strict and exhaustive definition of Lyrical Poetry ; but he has found the task of practical decision increase in clearness and in facility as he advanced with the work, whilst keeping in view a few simple principles. Lyrical has been here held essentially to imply that each Poem shall turn on some single thought, feeling, or situation. In accordance with this, narrative, descriptive, and didactic poems,—unless accompanied by rapidity of movement, brevity, and the colouring of human passion,—have been excluded. Humorous poetry, except in the very unfrequent instances where a truly poetical tone pervades the whole, with what is strictly personal, occasional, and religious, has been considered foreign to the idea of the book. Blank verse and the ten-syllable couplet, with all pieces markedly dramatic, have been rejected as alien from what is commonly understood by Song, and rarely conforming to Lyrical conditions in treatment. But it is not anticipated, nor is it possible, that all readers shall think the line accurately drawn. Some poems, as Gray's ' Elegy,' the ' Allegro ' and ' Penseroso,' Wordsworth's ' Ruth ' or Campbell's ' Lord Ullin,' might be claimed with perhaps equal justice for a narrative or descriptive selection : whilst with reference especially to Ballads and Sonnets, the Editor can only state that he has taken his utmost pains to decide without caprice or partiality.

This also is all he can plead in regard to a point even more liable to question ;—what degree of merit should give rank among the Best. That a Poem shall be worthy of the writer's genius,—that it shall reach a perfection commensurate with its aim,—that we should require finish in proportion to brevity,—that passion, colour, and originality cannot atone for serious imperfections in clearness, unity, or truth,—that a few good lines do not make a good poem,—that popular estimate is serviceable as a guidepost more than as a compass,—above all, that Excellence should be looked for rather in the Whole than in the Parts,—such and other such canons have been always steadily regarded. He may however add that the pieces chosen, and a far larger number rejected, have been carefully and repeatedly considered ; and that he has been aided throughout by two friends of independent and exercised judgement, besides the distinguished person addressed in the Dedication. It is hoped that by this procedure the volume has been freed from that onesidedness which must beset individual decisions :—but for the final choice the Editor is alone responsible.

It would obviously have been invidious to apply the standard aimed at in this Collection to the Living. Nor, even in the cases where this might be done without offence, does it appear wise to attempt to anticipate the verdict of the Future on our contemporaries. Should the book last, poems by Tennyson, Bryant, Clare, Lowell, and others, will no doubt claim and obtain their place among the best. But the Editor trusts that this will be effected by other hands, and in days far distant.

Chalmers' vast collection, with the whole works of all accessible poets not contained in it, and the best Anthologies of different periods, have been twice systematically read through : and it is hence improbable that any omissions which may be regretted are due to oversight. The poems are printed entire, except in a very few instances (specified in the notes) where a stanza has been omitted. The omissions have been risked only when the piece could be thus brought to a closer lyrical unity : and, as essentially opposed to this unity, extracts, obviously such, are excluded. In regard to the text, the purpose of the book has appeared to justify the choice of the most poetical version, wherever more than one exists : and much labour has been given to present each poem, in disposition, spelling, and punctuation, to the greatest advantage.

For the permission under which the copyright pieces are inserted, thanks are due to the respective Proprietors, without whose liberal concurrence the scheme of the collection would have been defeated.

In the arrangement, the most poetically-effective order has been attempted. The English mind has passed through phases of thought and cultivation so various and so opposed during these three centuries of Poetry, that a rapid passage between Old and New, like rapid alteration of the eye's focus in looking at the landscape, will always be wearisome and hurtful to the sense of Beauty. The poems have been therefore distributed into Books corresponding, I to the ninety years closing about 1616, II thence to 1700, III to 1800, IV to the half-century just ended. Or, looking at the Poets who more or less give each portion its distinctive character, they might be called the Books of Shakespeare, Milton, Gray, and Wordsworth. The volume, in this respect, so far as the limitations of its range allow, accurately reflects the natural growth and evolution of our Poetry.

A rigidly chronological sequence, however, rather fits a collection aiming at instruction than at pleasure, and the Wisdom which comes through Pleasure :—within each book the pieces have therefore been arranged in gradations of feeling or subject. The development of the symphonies of Mozart and Beethoven has been here thought of as a model, and nothing placed without careful consideration. And it is hoped that the contents of this Anthology will thus be found to present a certain unity, ' as episodes,' in the noble language of Shelley, ' to that great Poem which all poets, like the co-operating thoughts of one great mind, have built up since the beginning of the world.'

As he closes his long survey, the Editor trusts he may add without egotism, that he has found the vague general verdict of popular Fame more just than those have thought, who, with too severe a criticism, would confine judgements on Poetry to ' the selected few of many generations.' Not many appear to have gained reputation without some gift or performance that, in due degree, deserved it : and if no verses by certain writers who show less strength than sweetness, or more thought than mastery in expression, are printed in this volume, it should not be imagined that they have been excluded without much hesitation and regret,— far less that they have been slighted. Throughout this vast and pathetic array of Singers now silent, few have been honoured with the name Poet, and have not possessed a skill in words, a sympathy with beauty, a tenderness of feeling, or seriousness in reflection, which render their works, although never perhaps attaining that loftier and finer excellence here required,—better worth reading than much of what fills the scanty hours that most men spare for self-improvement, or for pleasure in any of its more elevated and permanent forms.— And if this be true of even mediocre poetry, for

how much more are we indebted to the best!
Like the fabled fountain of the Azores, but with
a more various power, the magic of this Art can
confer on each period of life its appropriate blessing:
on early years Experience, on maturity Calm, on
age Youthfulness. Poetry gives treasures 'more
golden than gold,' leading us in higher and healthier
ways than those of the world, and interpreting to
us the lessons of Nature. But she speaks best
for herself. Her true accents, if the plan has been
executed with success, may be heard throughout
the following pages :—wherever the Poets of
England are honoured, wherever the dominant
language of the world is spoken, it is hoped that
they will find fit audience.

F. T. P.

NOTE

Samuel Rogers, who died in 1855, was the last
poet included in *The Golden Treasury*. In this reprint additional poems are given representing the
poets since then to the present day. None but
Mr. Palgrave could have grouped the newer poems
in ' the most poetically-effective order ', as he con-
ceived it, so they have been added in the chronological order of their authors. A few dates in the
original selection have been corrected. Acknow-
ledgements for leave to include copyright poems
are due to Mr. Lascelles Abercrombie and Messrs.
John Lane for permission to include ' Margaret's
Song ' (from *Interludes and Poems*) ; Messrs. George
Bell & Sons for Mr. Coventry Patmore's ' The
Toys ' ; Mr. Laurence Binyon and The Times Pub-
lishing Co. for ' For the Fallen ' ; Messrs. William
Blackwood & Sons for George Eliot's ' O may I
join the choir invisible ' ; to Mr. Edmund Blunden
and Messrs. Sidgwick & Jackson for ' Alms-

women'; Mr. Robert Bridges for 'Gird on thy Sword', 'I have loved Flowers that Fade', and 'Nightingales'; Messrs. Burns, Oates & Washbourne, for Alice Meynell's 'Veneration of Images' and 'Unto Us', and for Francis Thompson's 'In No Strange Land'; Messrs. Chatto & Windus for Arthur O'Shaughnessy's ode and R. L. Stevenson's 'In Memoriam F. A. S.'; Mr. G. K. Chesterton and Messrs. Methuen for 'Before the Roman came to Rye' (from *The Flying Inn*); Messrs. Constable & Co. and Messrs. Charles Scribner's Sons, New York, for the four sonnets from George Meredith's 'Modern Love'; Messrs. John Lane for 'In Romney Marsh' (from *Ballads and Songs*); Mr. W. H. Davies and Messrs. Jonathan Cape for 'Sweet Stay-at-Home' (from *Collected Poems*); Mr. Walter de la Mare for 'Arabia' and 'Trees'; Mr. Alban Dobson for Austin Dobson's 'A Ballad to Queen Elizabeth'; Mr. John Drinkwater and Messrs. Sidgwick & Jackson for 'The Town Window'; Messrs. Elkin Mathews & Marrot for Lionel Johnson's 'Cadgwith'; the executors of the late Mr. J. E. Flecker and Messrs. Martin Secker for 'The Golden Journey to Samarkand'; Mrs. Henley and Mr. Nutt for Mr. W. E. Henley's 'Out of the night that covers me'; the family of Gerard Manley Hopkins and the Oxford University Press for 'Pied Beauty' and 'The Starlight Night'; Mr. A. E. Housman and Messrs. Grant Richards for 'An Epitaph on an Army of Mercenaries' (from *Last Poems*); Mr. Rudyard Kipling and Messrs. Methuen for 'Recessional' (from *The Five Nations*), 'The Last Chantey' (from *The Seven Seas*), and 'The Coward' (from *The Years Between*); Mr. John Masefield and Messrs. Heinemann for 'Sea-Fever' (from *Collected Poems*); Sir Henry Newbolt for 'Drake's Drum' and Mary Coleridge's 'We were Young'; Mr. J. D. C. Pellow and the Oxford University Press for 'London Bridge'; Mr. Siegfried Sassoon and Messrs. William Heinemann for 'Everyone Sang';

Messrs. Sidgwick & Jackson for Rupert Brooke's
'The Soldier'; the late Mr. Watts-Dunton for the
four poems by Swinburne; Mrs. Thomas for 'Adle-
strop' by Edward Thomas; Mr. Charles Williams
for 'After Ronsard'; Mr. W. B. Yeats and Messrs.
Macmillan for 'The Folly of being Comforted'
(from *Later Poems*); and Mr. W. B. Yeats and
Messrs. Ernest Benn for 'The Lake Isle of Innis-
free' (from *Poems*).

Additional thanks for other poems added in the
latest reprint are due to: Mr. W. H. Auden and
Messrs. Faber & Faber for 'Out on the Lawn',
'Look, Stranger' and 'A Shilling Life'; Mr. George
Barker and Messrs. Faber & Faber for 'The Seal
Boy' and 'The Chimera'; Mr. T. S. Eliot and Messrs.
Faber & Faber for 'Gerontion', 'Whispers of Immor-
tality' and 'Animula'; Mr. William Empson and
Messrs. Chatto & Windus for 'Description of a View'
and 'Note on Local Flora'; Mr. Cecil Day Lewis and
the Hogarth Press for 'The Flight' from *A Time to
Dance*; Mr. Louis MacNeice and Messrs. Faber &
Faber for 'Spring Voices' and 'Trapeze'; Mr. Wil-
fred Owen and Messrs. Chatto & Windus for
'Futility' and 'Strange Meeting'; Mr. Ezra Pound
for 'Lament of the Frontier Guard' and 'Villanelle:
The Psychological Hour'; Mr. John Crowe Ran-
som and Alfred A. Knopf Inc. for 'Necrological'
and 'Captain Carpenter' from *Chills and Fevers*;
Mr. Stephen Spender and Messrs. Faber & Faber
for 'How Strangely this Sun' and 'New Year';
Mr. Dylan Thomas for 'When once the Twilight'
and 'This Bread I Break'; Mrs. Yeats and Messrs.
Macmillan for 'A Prayer for my son', 'The Hawk',
'Byzantium', 'The Delphic Oracle Upon Plotinus',
'Two Songs of a Fool, II', 'From the "Antigone"'
(from *The Collected Poems of W. B. Yeats*).

THE GOLDEN TREASURY

BOOK FIRST

1

SPRING

Spring, the sweet Spring, is the year's pleasant
    king ;
Then blooms each thing, then maids dance in a ring,
Cold doth not sting, the pretty birds do sing,
    Cuckoo, jug-jug, pu-we, to-witta-woo !

The palm and may make country houses gay,   5
Lambs frisk and play, the shepherds pipe all day,
And we hear ay birds tune this merry lay,
    Cuckoo, jug-jug, pu-we, to-witta-woo !

The fields breathe sweet, the daisies kiss our feet,
Young lovers meet, old wives a-sunning sit,   10
In every street these tunes our ears do greet,
    Cuckoo, jug-jug, pu-we, to-witta-woo !
      Spring ! the sweet Spring !

T. Nash.

2

SUMMONS TO LOVE

    Phoebus, arise !
    And paint the sable skies
    With azure, white, and red :
Rouse Memnon's mother from her Tithon's bed
That she thy càreer may with roses spread :   5
The nightingales thy coming each-where sing :

Make an eternal spring,
Give life to this dark world which lieth dead ;
Spread forth thy golden hair
In larger locks than thou wast wont before,   10
And emperor-like decore
With diadem of pearl thy temples fair :
Chase hence the ugly night
Which serves but to make dear thy glorious light.

—This is that happy morn,   15
That day, long-wishèd day
Of all my life so dark,
(If cruel stars have not my ruin sworn
And fates my hopes betray),
Which, purely white, deserves   20
An everlasting diamond should it mark.
This is the morn should bring unto this grove
My Love, to hear and recompense my love.
Fair King, who all preserves,
But show thy blushing beams,   25
And thou two sweeter eyes
Shalt see than those which by Peneüs' streams
Did once thy heart surprise.
Now, Flora, deck thyself in fairest guise :
If that ye, winds, would hear   30
A voice surpassing far Amphion's lyre,
Your furious chiding stay ;
Let Zephyr only breathe,
And with her tresses play.
—The winds all silent are,   35
And Phoebus in his chair
Ensaffroning sea and air
Makes vanish every star :
Night like a drunkard reels
Beyond the hills, to shun his flaming wheels :   40
The fields with flowers are deck'd in every hue,
The clouds with orient gold spangle their blue ;
Here is the pleasant place—
And nothing wanting is, save She, alas !

W. DRUMMOND OF HAWTHORNDEN.

TIME AND LOVE

I

When I have seen by Time's fell hand defaced
  The rich proud cost of out-worn buried age ;
When sometime lofty towers I see down-razed,
  And brass eternal slave to mortal rage ;

When I have seen the hungry ocean gain   5
  Advantage on the kingdom of the shore,
And the firm soil win of the watery main,
  Increasing store with loss, and loss with store ;

When I have seen such interchange of state,
  Or state itself confounded to decay,   10
Ruin hath taught me thus to ruminate—
  That Time will come and take my Love away :

—This thought is as a death, which cannot choose
But weep to have that which it fears to lose.

                    W. SHAKESPEARE.

4

II

Since brass, nor stone, nor earth, nor boundless sea,
  But sad mortality o'ersways their power,
How with this rage shall beauty hold a plea,
  Whose action is no stronger than a flower ?

O how shall summer's honey breath hold out   5
  Against the wreckful siege of battering days,
When rocks impregnable are not so stout
  Nor gates of steel so strong, but time decays ?

O fearful meditation ! where, alack !   9
  Shall Time's best jewel from Time's chest lie hid?
Or what strong hand can hold his swift foot back,
  Or who his spoil of beauty can forbid ?

O ! none, unless this miracle have might,
That in black ink my love may still shine bright.

                    W. SHAKESPEARE.

5

THE PASSIONATE SHEPHERD TO HIS LOVE

Come live with me and be my Love,
And we will all the pleasures prove
That hills and valleys, dale and field,
And all the craggy mountains yield.

There will we sit upon the rocks   5
And see the shepherds feed their flocks,
By shallow rivers, to whose falls
Melodious birds sing madrigals.

There will I make thee beds of roses
And a thousand fragrant posies,   10
A cap of flowers, and a kirtle
Embroider'd all with leaves of myrtle.

A gown made of the finest wool,
Which from our pretty lambs we pull,
Fair linéd slippers for the cold,   15
With buckles of the purest gold.

A belt of straw and ivy buds
With coral clasps and amber studs :
And if these pleasures may thee move,
Come live with me and be my Love.   20

Thy silver dishes for thy meat
As precious as the gods do eat,
Shall on an ivory table be
Prepared each day for thee and me.

The shepherd swains shall dance and sing   25
For thy delight each May-morning :
If these delights thy mind may move,
Then live with me and be my Love.

C. MARLOWE.

6

A MADRIGAL

Crabbed Age and Youth
Cannot live together :
  Youth is full of pleasance,
Age is full of care ;
  Youth like summer morn, 5
Age like winter weather,
  Youth like summer brave,
Age like winter bare :
  Youth is full of sport,
  Age's breath is short, 10
Youth is nimble, Age is lame :
  Youth is hot and bold,
  Age is weak and cold,
Youth is wild, and Age is tame :—
  Age, I do abhor thee, 15
  Youth, I do adore thee ;
O ! my Love, my Love is young !
  Age, I do defy thee—
  O sweet shepherd, hie thee,
For methinks thou stay'st too long. 20

W. SHAKESPEARE.

7

Under the greenwood tree
Who loves to lie with me,
And turn his merry note
Unto the sweet bird's throat—
Come hither, come hither, come hither ! 5
  Here shall he see
  No enemy
But winter and rough weather.

Who doth ambition shun
And loves to live i' the sun, 10

Seeking the food he eats
  And pleased with what he gets—
Come hither, come hither, come hither !
    Here shall he see
    No enemy   15
But winter and rough weather.

W. SHAKESPEARE.

8

It was a lover and his lass
  With a hey and a ho, and a hey-nonino !
That o'er the green cornfield did pass
In the spring time, the only pretty ring time,
When birds do sing hey ding a ding ding : 5
  Sweet lovers love the Spring.

Between the acres of the rye
These pretty country folks would lie :

This carol they began that hour,
How that a life was but a flower :   10

And therefore take the present time
  With a hey and a ho, and a hey-nonino !
For love is crownéd with the prime
In spring time, the only pretty ring time,
When birds do sing hey ding a ding ding :
  Sweet lovers love the Spring.   16

W. SHAKESPEARE.

9

PRESENT IN ABSENCE

Absence, hear thou my protestation
    Against thy strength,
    Distance, and length ;
Do what thou canst for alteration :

For hearts of truest mettle 5
Absence doth join, and Time doth settle.

Who loves a mistress of such quality,
He soon hath found
Affection's ground
Beyond time, place, and all mortality. 10
To hearts that cannot vary
Absence is Present, Time doth tarry.

By absence this good means I gain,
That I can catch her,
Where none can watch her, 15
In some close corner of my brain :
There I embrace and kiss her ;
And so I both enjoy and miss her.

ANON.

10

ABSENCE

Being your slave, what should I do but tend
Upon the hours and times of your desire ?
I have no precious time at all to spend
Nor services to do, till you require :

Nor dare I chide the world-without-end hour 5
Whilst I, my sovereign, watch the clock for you,
Nor think the bitterness of absence sour
When you have bid your servant once adieu :

Nor dare I question with my jealous thought
Where you may be, or your affairs suppose, 10
But like a sad slave, stay and think of nought
Save, where you are, how happy you make
those ;—

So true a fool is love, that in your will,
Though you do anything, he thinks no ill.

W. SHAKESPEARE.

11

How like a winter hath my absence been
 From Thee, the pleasure of the fleeting year !
What freezings have I felt, what dark days seen,
 What old December's bareness everywhere !

And yet this time removed was summer's time ; 5
 The teeming autumn, big with rich increase,
Bearing the wanton burden of the prime
 Like widow'd wombs after their lords' decease :

Yet this abundant issue seem'd to me
 But hope of orphans, and unfather'd fruit ; 10
For summer and his pleasures wait on thee,
 And, thou away, the very birds are mute ;

Or if they sing, 'tis with so dull a cheer,
That leaves look pale, dreading the winter's near.
       W. Shakespeare.

12

A CONSOLATION

When in disgrace with fortune and men's eyes
 I all alone beweep my outcast state,
And trouble deaf heaven with my bootless cries,
 And look upon myself, and curse my fate :

Wishing me like to one more rich in hope, 5
 Featured like him, like him with friends possest,
Desiring this man's art, and that man's scope,
 With what I most enjoy contented least ;

Yet in these thoughts myself almost despising,
 Haply I think on Thee—and then my state, 10
Like to the lark at break of day arising
 From sullen earth, sings hymns at heaven's gate ;

For thy sweet love remember'd such wealth brings,
That then I scorn to change my state with kings.
       W. Shakespeare.

13

THE UNCHANGEABLE

O never say that I was false of heart,
  Though absence seem'd my flame to qualify :
As easy might I from myself depart
  As from my soul, which in thy breast doth lie ;

That is my home of love ; if I have ranged,   5
  Like him that travels, I return again.
Just to the time, not with the time exchanged,
  So that myself bring water for my stain.

Never believe, though in my nature reign'd
  All frailties that besiege all kinds of blood,   10
That it could so preposterously be stain'd
  To leave for nothing all thy sum of good :

For nothing this wide universe I call,
Save thou, my rose : in it thou art my all.

                    W. SHAKESPEARE.

14

To me, fair Friend, you never can be old,
  For as you were when first your eye I eyed
Such seems your beauty still. Three winters cold
  Have from the forests shook three summers'
    pride ;

Three beauteous springs to yellow autumn turn'd 5
  In process of the seasons have I seen,
Three April perfumes in three hot Junes burn'd,
  Since first I saw you fresh, which yet are green.

Ah ! yet doth beauty, like a dial-hand,
  Steal from his figure, and no pace perceived ;   10
So your sweet hue, which methinks still doth stand,
  Hath motion, and mine eye may be deceived :

For fear of which, hear this, thou age unbred,—
Ere you were born, was beauty's summer dead.

                    W. SHAKESPEARE.

15

DIAPHENIA

Diaphenia like the daffadowndilly,
  White as the sun, fair as the lily,
Heigh ho, how I do love thee !
    I do love thee as my lambs
    Are belovéd of their dams ;   5
How blest were I if thou would'st prove me.

Diaphenia like the spreading roses,
  That in thy sweets all sweets encloses,
Fair sweet, how I do love thee !
    I do love thee as each flower   10
    Loves the sun's life-giving power ;
For dead, thy breath to life might move me.

Diaphenia like to all things blesséd
  When all thy praises are expresséd,
Dear joy, how I do love thee !   15
    As the birds do love the spring,
    Or the bees their careful king :
Then in requite, sweet virgin, love me !

                   H. CONSTABLE.

16

ROSALYNDE

Like to the clear in highest sphere
  Where all imperial glory shines,
Of selfsame colour is her hair
  Whether unfolded, or in twines :
    Heigh ho, fair Rosalynde !   5
Her eyes are sapphires set in snow,
  Resembling heaven by every wink ;
The Gods do fear whenas they glow,
  And I do tremble when I think
    Heigh ho, would she were mine !   10

Her cheeks are like the blushing cloud
  That beautifies Aurora's face,
Or like the silver crimson shroud
  That Phoebus' smiling looks doth grace ;
    Heigh ho, fair Rosalynde !   15
Her lips are like two budded roses
  Whom ranks of lilies neighbour nigh,
Within which bounds she balm encloses
  Apt to entice a deity :
    Heigh ho, would she were mine !   20

Her neck is like a stately tower
  Where Love himself imprison'd lies,
To watch for glances every hour
  From her divine and sacred eyes :
    Heigh ho, for Rosalynde !   25
Her paps are centres of delight,
  Her breasts are orbs of heavenly frame,
Where Nature moulds the dew of light
  To feed perfection with the same :
    Heigh ho, would she were mine !   30

With orient pearl, with ruby red,
  With marble white, with sapphire blue
Her body every way is fed,
  Yet soft in touch and sweet in view :
    Heigh ho, fair Rosalynde !   35
Nature herself her shape admires ;
  The Gods are wounded in her sight ;
And Love forsakes his heavenly fires
  And at her eyes his brand doth light :
    Heigh ho, would she were mine !   40

Then muse not, Nymphs, though I bemoan
  The absence of fair Rosalynde,
Since for a fair there's fairer none,
  Nor for her virtues so divine :
    Heigh ho, fair Rosalynde ;   45
Heigh ho, my heart ! would God that she were
mine !
                  T. LODGE.

17

COLIN

Beauty sat bathing by a spring
    Where fairest shades did hide her ;
The winds blew calm, the birds did sing,
    The cool streams ran beside her.
My wanton thoughts enticed mine eye   5
    To see what was forbidden :
But better memory said, fie !
    So vain desire was chidden :—
        Hey nonny nonny O !
        Hey nonny nonny !   10

Into a slumber then I fell,
    When fond imagination
Seem'd to see, but could not tell
    Her feature or her fashion.
But ev'n as babes in dreams do smile,   15
    And sometimes fall a-weeping,
So I awaked, as wise this while
    As when I fell a-sleeping :—
        Hey nonny nonny O !
        Hey nonny nonny !   20
            THE SHEPHERD TONY.

18

TO HIS LOVE

Shall I compare thee to a summer's day ?
    Thou art more lovely and more temperate :
Rough winds do shake the darling buds of May,
    And summer's lease hath all too short a date :

Sometime too hot the eye of heaven shines,   5
    And often is his gold complexion dimm'd :
And every fair from fair sometime declines,
    By chance, or nature's changing course, un-
        trimm'd.

But thy eternal summer shall not fade
  Nor lose possession of that fair thou owest ;   10
Nor shall death brag thou wanderest in his shade,
  When in eternal lines to time thou growest :

So long as men can breathe, or eyes can see,
So long lives this, and this gives life to thee.

W. SHAKESPEARE.

19

TO HIS LOVE

When in the chronicle of wasted time
  I see descriptions of the fairest wights,
And beauty making beautiful old rhyme
  In praise of ladies dead, and lovely knights ;

Then in the blazon of sweet beauty's best   5
  Of hand, of foot, of lip, of eye, of brow,
I see their antique pen would have exprest
  Ev'n such a beauty as you master now.

So all their praises are but prophecies
  Of this our time, all you prefiguring ;   10
And, for they look'd but with divining eyes,
  They had not skill enough your worth to sing :

For we, which now behold these present days,
Have eyes to wonder but lack tongues to praise.

W. SHAKESPEARE.

20

LOVE'S PERJURIES

On a day, alack the day !
Love, whose month is ever May,
Spied a blossom passing fair
Playing in the wanton air :
Through the velvet leaves the wind,   5
All unseen, 'gan passage find ;

That the lover, sick to death,
Wish'd himself the heaven's breath.
Air, quoth he, thy cheeks may blow ;
Air, would I might triumph so !   10
But, alack, my hand is sworn
Ne'er to pluck thee from thy thorn :
Vow, alack, for youth unmeet ;
Youth so apt to pluck a sweet.
Do not call it sin in me   15
That I am forsworn for thee :
Thou for whom Jove would swear
Juno but an Ethiope were,
And deny himself for Jove,
Turning mortal for thy love.   20

                              W. SHAKESPEARE.

21

A SUPPLICATION

Forget not yet the tried intent
Of such a truth as I have meant ;
My great travail so gladly spent,
          Forget not yet !

Forget not yet when first began   5
The weary life ye know, since whan
The suit, the service none tell can ;
          Forget not yet !

Forget not yet the great assays,
The cruel wrong, the scornful ways,   10
The painful patience in delays,
          Forget not yet !

Forget not ! O, forget not this,
How long ago hath been, and is
The mind that never meant amiss—   15
          Forget not yet !

Were you the earth, dear Love, and I the skies,
My love should shine on you like to the sun,   10
And look upon you with ten thousand eyes
Till heaven wax'd blind, and till the world were
done.

Wheresoe'er I am, below, or else above you,
Wheresoe'er you are, my heart shall truly love you.

J. SYLVESTER.

26

CARPE DIEM

O Mistress mine, where are you roaming ?
O stay and hear ! your true-love's coming
   That can sing both high and low ;
Trip no further, pretty sweeting,
Journeys end in lovers' meeting—   5
   Every wise man's son doth know.

What is love ? 'tis not hereafter ;
Present mirth hath present laughter ;
   What's to come is still unsure :
In delay there lies no plenty,—   10
Then come kiss me, Sweet-and-twenty,
   Youth's a stuff will not endure.

W. SHAKESPEARE.

27

WINTER

When icicles hang by the wall
   And Dick the shepherd blows his nail,
And Tom bears logs into the hall,
   And milk comes frozen home in pail ;
When blood is nipt, and ways be foul,   5
Then nightly sings the staring owl
      Tuwhoo !
Tuwhit ! tuwhoo ! A merry note !
While greasy Joan doth keel the pot.

When all aloud the wind doth blow,   10
  And coughing drowns the parson's saw,
And birds sit brooding in the snow,
  And Marian's nose looks red and raw ;
When roasted crabs hiss in the bowl—
Then nightly sings the staring owl   15
        Tuwhoo !
Tuwhit ! tuwhoo ! A merry note !
While greasy Joan doth keel the pot.

                 W. SHAKESPEARE.

28

That time of year thou may'st in me behold
  When yellow leaves, or none, or few, do hang
Upon those boughs which shake against the cold,
  Bare ruin'd choirs, where late the sweet birds
    sang.

In me thou see'st the twilight of such day   5
  As after sunset fadeth in the west,
Which by and by black night doth take away,
  Death's second self, that seals up all in rest.

In me thou see'st the glowing of such fire,
  That on the ashes of his youth doth lie   10
As the death-bed whereon it must expire,
  Consumed with that which it was nourish'd by :

—This thou perceiv'st, which makes thy love more
    strong,
To love that well which thou must leave ere long.

                 W. SHAKESPEARE.

29

REMEMBRANCE

When to the sessions of sweet silent thought
  I summon up remembrance of things past,
I sigh the lack of many a thing I sought,
  And with old woes new wail my dear time's
    waste ;

Then can I drown an eye, unused to flow,   5
  For precious friends hid in death's dateless night,
And weep afresh love's long-since-cancell'd woe,
  And moan the expense of many a vanish'd sight.

Then can I grieve at grievances foregone,
  And heavily from woe to woe tell o'er   10
The sad account of fore-bemoanéd moan,
  Which I new pay as if not paid before :

—But if the while I think on thee, dear friend,
All losses are restored, and sorrows end.

W. SHAKESPEARE.

30

REVOLUTIONS

Like as the waves make towards the pebbled shore,
  So do our minutes hasten to their end ;
Each changing place with that which goes before,
  In sequent toil all forwards do contend.

Nativity, once in the main of light,   5
  Crawls to maturity, wherewith being crown'd,
Crooked eclipses 'gainst his glory fight,
  And Time that gave doth now his gift confound.

Time doth transfix the flourish set on youth,
  And delves the parallels in beauty's brow ;   10
Feeds on the rarities of nature's truth,
  And nothing stands but for his scythe to mow :

And yet, to times in hope, my verse shall stand
Praising thy worth, despite his cruel hand.

W. SHAKESPEARE.

31

Farewell ! thou art too dear for my possessing,
  And like enough thou know'st thy estimate :
The charter of thy worth gives thee releasing ;
  My bonds in thee are all determinate.

For how do I hold thee but by thy granting?   5
  And for that riches where is my deserving?
The cause of this fair gift in me is wanting,
  And so my patent back again is swerving.

Thyself thou gav'st, thy own worth then not
      knowing,   9
  Or me, to whom thou gav'st it, else mistaking;
So thy great gift, upon misprision growing,
  Comes home again, on better judgement making.

Thus have I had thee as a dream doth flatter;
In sleep, a king; but waking, no such matter.

W. SHAKESPEARE.

32

THE LIFE WITHOUT PASSION

They that have power to hurt, and will do none,
  That do not do the thing they most do show,
Who, moving others, are themselves as stone,
  Unmovéd, cold, and to temptation slow,—

They rightly do inherit Heaven's graces,   5
  And husband nature's riches from expense;
They are the lords and owners of their faces,
  Others, but stewards of their excellence.

The summer's flower is to the summer sweet,
  Though to itself it only live and die;   10
But if that flower with base infection meet,
  The basest weed outbraves his dignity:

For sweetest things turn sourest by their deeds;
Lilies that fester smell far worse than weeds.

W. SHAKESPEARE.

33

THE LOVER'S APPEAL

And wilt thou leave me thus?
  Say nay! say nay! for shame!
  To save thee from the blame
  Of all my grief and grame.
And wilt thou leave me thus?   5
  Say nay! say nay!

And wilt thou leave me thus,
  That hath loved thee so long
  In wealth and woe among?
  And is thy heart so strong   10
As for to leave me thus?
  Say nay! say nay!

And wilt thou leave me thus,
  That hath given thee my heart
  Never for to depart   15
  Neither for pain nor smart?
And wilt thou leave me thus?
  Say nay! say nay!

And wilt thou leave me thus,
  And have no more pity   20
  Of him that loveth thee?
  Alas! thy cruelty!
And wilt thou leave me thus?
  Say nay! say nay!

SIR T. WYATT.

34

THE NIGHTINGALE

As it fell upon a day
In the merry month of May,
Sitting in a pleasant shade
Which a grove of myrtles made,

Beasts did leap and birds did sing,   5
Trees did grow and plants did spring,
Every thing did banish moan
Save the Nightingale alone.
She, poor bird, as all forlorn,
Lean'd her breast up-till a thorn,   10
And there sung the dolefull'st ditty
That to hear it was great pity.
Fie, fie, fie, now would she cry;
Tereu, tereu, by and by:
That to hear her so complain   15
Scarce I could from tears refrain;
For her griefs so lively shown
Made me think upon mine own.
—Ah, thought I, thou mourn'st in vain,
None takes pity on thy pain: 20
Senseless trees, they cannot hear thee,
Ruthless beasts, they will not cheer thee;
King Pandion, he is dead,
All thy friends are lapp'd in lead:
All thy fellow birds do sing   25
Careless of thy sorrowing:
Even so, poor bird, like thee
None alive will pity me.

R. BARNFIELD.

35

Care-charmer Sleep, son of the sable Night,
  Brother to Death, in silent darkness born,
Relieve my languish, and restore the light;
  With dark forgetting of my care return.

And let the day be time enough to mourn   5
The shipwreck of my ill-adventured youth:
  Let waking eyes suffice to wail their scorn,
Without the torment of the night's untruth.

Cease, dreams, the images of day-desires,   9
  To model forth the passions of the morrow;

Never let rising Sun approve you liars
    To add more grief to aggravate my sorrow :

Still let me sleep, embracing clouds in vain,
And never wake to feel the day's disdain.

S. DANIEL.

36
MADRIGAL

Take, O take those lips away
    That so sweetly were forsworn,
And those eyes, the break of day,
    Lights that do mislead the morn :
But my kisses bring again,   5
        Bring again—
Seals of love, but seal'd in vain,
        Seal'd in vain !

W. SHAKESPEARE.

37
LOVE'S FAREWELL

Since there's no help, come let us kiss and part,—
    Nay I have done, you get no more of me ;
And I am glad, yea, glad with all my heart,
    That thus so cleanly I myself can free ;

Shake hands for ever, cancel all our vows,   5
    And when we meet at any time again,
Be it not seen in either of our brows
    That we one jot of former love retain.

Now at the last gasp of love's latest breath,
    When, his pulse failing, passion speechless lies, 10
When faith is kneeling by his bed of death,
    And innocence is closing up his eyes,

—Now if thou would'st, when all have given him
        over,
From death to life thou might'st him yet recover !

M. DRAYTON.

38

TO HIS LUTE

My lute, be as thou wert when thou didst grow
  With thy green mother in some shady grove,
  When immelodious winds but made thee move,
And birds their ramage did on thee bestow.

  Since that dear Voice which did thy sounds
    approve,   5
Which wont in such harmonious strains to flow,
  Is reft from Earth to tune those spheres above,
What art thou but a harbinger of woe ?

Thy pleasing notes be pleasing notes no more,
  But orphans' wailings to the fainting ear ;   10
  Each stroke a sigh, each sound draws forth a
    tear ;
For which be silent as in woods before :
Or if that any hand to touch thee deign,
Like widow'd turtle still her loss complain.

                  W. DRUMMOND.

39

BLIND LOVE

O me ! what eyes hath love put in my head
  Which have no correspondence with true sight :
Or if they have, where is my judgement fled
  That censures falsely what they see aright ?

If that be fair whereon my false eyes dote,   5
  What means the world to say it is not so ?
If it be not, then love doth well denote
  Love's eye is not so true as all men's : No,

How can it ?   O how can love's eye be true,   9
  That is so vex'd with watching and with tears ?
No marvel then though I mistake my view :
  The sun itself sees not till heaven clears.

O cunning Love ! with tears thou keep'st me blind,
Lest eyes well-seeing thy foul faults should find !

                  W. SHAKESPEARE.

40

THE UNFAITHFUL SHEPHERDESS

While that the sun with his beams hot
  Scorchéd the fruits in vale and mountain,
Philon the shepherd, late forgot,
  Sitting beside a crystal fountain,
    In shadow of a green oak tree   5
    Upon his pipe this song play'd he :
Adieu Love, adieu Love, untrue Love,
Untrue Love, untrue Love, adieu Love ;
Your mind is light, soon lost for new love.

So long as I was in your sight   10
  I was your heart, your soul, and treasure ;
And evermore you sobb'd and sigh'd
  Burning in flames beyond all measure :
    —Three days endured your love to me,
    And it was lost in other three !   15
Adieu Love, adieu Love, untrue Love,
Untrue Love, untrue Love, adieu Love ;
Your mind is light, soon lost for new love.

Another Shepherd you did see
  To whom your heart was soon enchainéd ;
Full soon your love was leapt from me,   21
  Full soon my place he had obtainéd.
    Soon came a third, your love to win,
    And we were out and he was in.
Adieu Love, adieu Love, untrue Love,   25
Untrue Love, untrue Love, adieu Love ;
Your mind is light, soon lost for new love.

Sure you have made me passing glad
  That you your mind so soon removéd,
Before that I the leisure had   30
  To choose you for my best belovéd :

For all your love was past and done
Two days before it was begun :—
Adieu Love, adieu Love, untrue Love,
Untrue Love, untrue Love, adieu Love ;   35
Your mind is light, soon lost for new love.

ANON.

41

A RENUNCIATION

If women could be fair, and yet not fond,
  Or that their love were firm, not fickle still,
I would not marvel that they make men bond
  By service long to purchase their good will ;
But when I see how frail those creatures are,   5
I muse that men forget themselves so far.

To mark the choice they make, and how they change,
  How oft from Phoebus they do flee to Pan ;
Unsettled still, like haggards wild they range,
  These gentle birds that fly from man to man ;   10
Who would not scorn and shake them from the fist,
And let them fly, fair fools, which way they list ?

Yet for disport we fawn and flatter both,
  To pass the time when nothing else can please,
And train them to our lure with subtle oath,   15
  Till, weary of their wiles, ourselves we ease ;
And then we say when we their fancy try,
To play with fools, O what a fool was I !

E. VERE, EARL OF OXFORD.

42

Blow, blow, thou winter wind,
Thou art not so unkind
  As man's ingratitude ;
Thy tooth is not so keen
Because thou art not seen,   5
  Although thy breath be rude.

Heigh ho ! sing heigh ho ! unto the green holly :
Most friendship is feigning, most loving mere folly :
    Then, heigh ho ! the holly !
    This life is most jolly.   10

    Freeze, freeze, thou bitter sky,
    That dost not bite so nigh
      As benefits forgot :
    Though thou the waters warp,
    Thy sting is not so sharp   15
      As friend remember'd not.
Heigh ho ! sing heigh ho ! unto the green holly :
Most friendship is feigning, most loving mere folly :
    Then, heigh ho ! the holly !
    This life is most jolly.   20

              W. SHAKESPEARE.

43

MADRIGAL

My thoughts hold mortal strife
I do detest my life,
  And with lamenting cries,
  Peace to my soul to bring,
Oft call that prince which here doth monarchize : 5
—But he, grim grinning King,
Who caitiffs scorns, and doth the blest surprise,
Late having deck'd with beauty's rose his tomb,
Disdains to crop a weed, and will not come.

              W. DRUMMOND.

44

DIRGE OF LOVE

Come away, come away, Death,
  And in sad cypres let me be laid ;
Fly away, fly away, breath ;
  I am slain by a fair cruel maid.

My shroud of white, stuck all with yew,   5
  O prepare it !
My part of death, no one so true
  Did share it.

 Not a flower, not a flower sweet
On my black coffin let there be strown ;   10
 Not a friend, not a friend greet
My poor corpse, where my bones shall be thrown :
A thousand thousand sighs to save,
  Lay me, O where
Sad true lover never find my grave,   15
  To weep there.
      W. SHAKESPEARE.

45

FIDELE

Fear no more the heat o' the sun
  Nor the furious winter's rages ;
Thou thy worldly task hast done,
  Home art gone and ta'en thy wages :
Golden lads and girls all must,   5
As chimney-sweepers, come to dust.

Fear no more the frown o' the great,
  Thou art past the tyrant's stroke ;
Care no more to clothe and eat ;
  To thee the reed is as the oak :   10
The sceptre, learning, physic, must
All follow this, and come to dust.

Fear no more the lightning-flash
  Nor the all-dreaded thunder-stone ;
Fear not slander, censure rash ;   15
  Thou hast finish'd joy and moan :
All lovers young, all lovers must
Consign to thee, and come to dust.
      W. SHAKESPEARE.

46

A SEA DIRGE

Full fathom five thy father lies :
  Of his bones are coral made ;
Those are pearls that were his eyes :
  Nothing of him that doth fade
But doth suffer a sea-change   5
Into something rich and strange.
Sea-nymphs hourly ring his knell :
Hark ! now I hear them,—
    Ding, dong, bell.

            W. SHAKESPEARE.

47

A LAND DIRGE

Call for the robin-redbreast and the wren,
  Since o'er shady groves they hover
  And with leaves and flowers do cover
The friendless bodies of unburied men.
  Call unto his funeral dole   5
  The ant, the field-mouse, and the mole,
To rear him hillocks that shall keep him warm
And (when gay tombs are robb'd) sustain no harm ;
But keep the wolf far thence, that's foe to men,
For with his nails he'll dig them up again.   10

            J. WEBSTER.

48

POST MORTEM

If thou survive my well-contented day
  When that churl Death my bones with dust shall
    cover,
And shalt by fortune once more re-survey
  These poor rude lines of thy deceaséd lover ;

Compare them with the bettering of the time, 5
  And though they be outstripp'd by every pen,
Reserve them for my love, not for their rhyme
  Exceeded by the height of happier men.

O then vouchsafe me but this loving thought—
  ' Had my friend's muse grown with this growing
    age, 10
A dearer birth than this his love had brought,
  To march in ranks of better equipage :

But since he died, and poets better prove,
Theirs for their style I'll read, his for his love.'

W. SHAKESPEARE.

49

THE TRIUMPH OF DEATH

No longer mourn for me when I am dead
  Than you shall hear the surly sullen bell
Give warning to the world, that I am fled
  From this vile world, with vilest worms to dwell ;
Nay, if you read this line, remember not 5
  The hand that writ it ; for I love you so,
That I in your sweet thoughts would be forgot
  If thinking on me then should make you woe.
O if, I say, you look upon this verse
  When I perhaps compounded am with clay, 10
Do not so much as my poor name rehearse,
  But let your love even with my life decay ;
Lest the wise world should look into your moan,
And mock you with me after I am gone.

W. SHAKESPEARE.

50

MADRIGAL

Tell me where is Fancy bred,
  Or in the heart, or in the head ?
How begot, how nourishéd ?
  Reply, reply.

It is engender'd in the eyes,   5
With gazing fed ; and Fancy dies
In the cradle where it lies :
    Let us all ring Fancy's knell ;
    I'll begin it,—Ding, dong, bell.
        —Ding, dong, bell.   10

                  W. SHAKESPEARE.

51
CUPID AND CAMPASPE

Cupid and my Campaspe play'd
At cards for kisses ; Cupid paid :
He stakes his quiver, bow, and arrows,
His mother's doves, and team of sparrows ;
Loses them too ; then down he throws   5
The coral of his lip, the rose
Growing on 's cheek (but none knows how) ;
With these, the crystal of his brow,
And then the dimple of his chin ;
All these did my Campaspe win :   10
At last he set her both his eyes—
She won, and Cupid blind did rise.
    O Love ! has she done this to thee ?
    What shall, alas ! become of me ?

                    J. LYLY.

52

Pack, clouds, away, and welcome day,
  With night we banish sorrow ;
Sweet air blow soft, mount lark aloft
  To give my Love good-morrow !
Wings from the wind to please her mind   5
  Notes from the lark I'll borrow ;
Bird prune thy wing, nightingale sing,
  To give my Love good-morrow ;
    To give my Love good-morrow
    Notes from them all I'll borrow.   10

Wake from thy nest, Robin-red-breast,
  Sing birds in every furrow ;
And from each bill, let music shrill
  Give my fair Love good-morrow !
Blackbird and thrush in every bush,   15
  Stare, linnet, and cock-sparrow,
You pretty elves, amongst yourselves
  Sing my fair Love good-morrow !
    To give my Love good-morrow
    Sing birds in every furrow !   20

                   T. HEYWOOD.

53

PROTHALAMION

Calm was the day, and through the trembling air
  Sweet-breathing Zephyrus did softly play—
A gentle spirit, that lightly did delay
Hot Titan's beams, which then did glister fair ;
  When I (whom sullen care,   5
Through discontent of my long fruitless stay
In princes' court, and expectation vain
Of idle hopes, which still do fly away
  Like empty shadows, did afflict my brain)
    Walk'd forth to ease my pain   10
Along the shore of silver-streaming Thames ;
  Whose rutty bank, the which his river hems,
  Was painted all with variable flowers,
And all the meads adorn'd with dainty gems
    Fit to deck maidens' bowers,   15
    And crown their paramours
Against the bridal day, which is not long :
Sweet Thames ! run softly, till I end my song.

There in a meadow by the river's side
  A flock of nymphs I chancéd to espy,   20
  All lovely daughters of the flood thereby,
With goodly greenish locks all loose untied
    As each had been a bride ;

And each one had a little wicker basket
  Made of fine twigs, entrailéd curiously,   25
In which they gather'd flowers to fill their flasket,
    And with fine fingers cropt full feateously
      The tender stalks on high.
Of every sort which in that meadow grew
They gather'd some ; the violet, pallid blue,   30
  The little daisy that at evening closes,
The virgin lily and the primrose true,
    With store of vermeil roses,
    To deck their bridegrooms' posies
Against the bridal day, which was not long :   35
Sweet Thames ! run softly, till I end my song.

With that I saw two swans of goodly hue
  Come softly swimming down along the lee ;
  Two fairer birds I yet did never see ;
The snow which doth the top of Pindus strow   40
  Did never whiter show,
Nor Jove himself, when he a swan would be
  For love of Leda, whiter did appear ;
Yet Leda was (they say) as white as he,   44
  Yet not so white as these, nor nothing near ;
    So purely white they were,
That even the gentle stream, the which them bare,
Seem'd foul to them, and bade his billows spare
  To wet their silken feathers, lest they might
Soil their fair plumes with water not so fair,   50
    And mar their beauties bright,
    That shone as Heaven's light
Against their bridal day, which was not long :
Sweet Thames ! run softly, till I end my song.

Eftsoons the nymphs, which now had flowers their fill,
  Ran all in haste to see that silver brood   56
  As they came floating on the crystal flood ;
Whom when they saw, they stood amazéd still
    Their wondering eyes to fill ;
Them seem'd they never saw a sight so fair   60
  Of fowls, so lovely, that they sure did deem
Them heavenly born, or to be that same pair

Which through the sky draw Venus' silver team ;
For sure they did not seem
To be begot of any earthly seed, 65
But rather angels, or of angels' breed ;
Yet were they bred of summer's heat, they say,
In sweetest season, when each flower and weed
The earth did fresh array ;
So fresh they seem'd as day, 70
Even as their bridal day, which was not long :
Sweet Thames ! run softly, till I end my song.

Then forth they all out of their baskets drew
Great store of flowers, the honour of the field,
That to the sense did fragrant odours yield, 75
All which upon those goodly birds they threw
And all the waves did strew,
That like old Peneus' waters they did seem
When down along by pleasant Tempe's shore
Scatter'd with flowers, through Thessaly they
stream, 80
That they appear, through lilies' plenteous store,
Like a bride's chamber-floor.
Two of those nymphs meanwhile two garlands bound
Of freshest flowers which in that mead they found,
The which presenting all in trim array, 85
Their snowy foreheads therewithal they crown'd ;
Whilst one did sing this lay
Prepared against that day,
Against their bridal day, which was not long :
Sweet Thames ! run softly, till I end my song. 90

' Ye gentle birds ! the world's fair ornament,
And Heaven's glory, whom this happy hour
Doth lead unto your lovers' blissful bower,
Joy may you have, and gentle heart's content
Of your love's couplement ; 95
And let fair Venus, that is queen of love,
With her heart-quelling son upon you smile,
Whose smile, they say, hath virtue to remove
All love's dislike, and friendship's faulty guile
For ever to assoil. 100

Let endless peace your steadfast hearts accord,
And blessed plenty wait upon your board ;
 And let your bed with pleasures chaste abound,
That fruitful issue may to you afford
  Which may your foes confound, 105
  And make your joys redound
Upon your bridal day, which is not long :
Sweet Thames ! run softly, till I end my song.'

So ended she ; and all the rest around
 To her redoubled that her undersong, 110
 Which said their bridal day should not be long :
And gentle Echo from the neighbour ground
 Their accents did resound.
So forth those joyous birds did pass along 114
 Adown the lee that to them murmur'd low,
As he would speak but that he lack'd a tongue,
 Yet did by signs his glad affection show,
  Making his stream run slow.
And all the fowl which in his flood did dwell
'Gan flock about these twain, that did excel 120
 The rest, so far as Cynthia doth shend
The lesser stars. So they, enrangéd well,
  Did on those two attend,
  And their best service lend 124
Against their wedding day, which was not long :
Sweet Thames ! run softly, till I end my song.

At length they all to merry London came,
 To merry London, my most kindly nurse,
That to me gave this life's first native source,
Though from another place I take my name, 130
  An house of ancient fame :
There when they came whereas those bricky towers
 The which on Thames' broad aged back do ride,
Where now the studious lawyers have their bowers,
 There whilome wont the Templar-knights to
  bide, 135
  Till they decay'd through pride ;
Next whereunto there stands a stately place,
Where oft I gainéd gifts and goodly grace

Of that great lord, which therein wont to dwell,
Whose want too well now feels my friendless case ;
　　　But ah ! here fits not well　　　　　141
　　　Old woes, but joys, to tell
Against the bridal day, which is not long :
Sweet Thames ! run softly, till I end my song.

Yet therein now doth lodge a noble peer,　　145
　　　Great England's glory and the world's wide
　　　　　wonder,
　　Whose dreadful name late through all Spain did
　　　　　thunder,
And Hercules' two pillars standing near
　　　Did make to quake and fear :
Fair branch of honour, flower of chivalry !　　150
　　　That fillest England with thy triumphs' fame,
Joy have thou of thy noble victory,
　　And endless happiness of thine own name
　　　That promiseth the same ;
That through thy prowess and victorious arms　155
Thy country may be freed from foreign harms,
　　And great Eliza's glorious name may ring
Through all the world, fill'd with thy wide alarms,
　　　Which some brave Muse may sing
　　　To ages following,　　　　　　　160
Upon the bridal day, which is not long :
Sweet Thames ! run softly, till I end my song.

From those high towers this noble lord issúing
　　Like radiant Hesper, when his golden hair
　　In th' ocean billows he hath bathéd fair,　　165
Descended to the river's open viewing
　　With a great train ensuing.
Above the rest were goodly to be seen
　　Two gentle knights of lovely face and feature,
Beseeming well the bower of any queen,　　170
　　　With gifts of wit and ornaments of nature,
　　　Fit for so goodly stature,
That like the twins of Jove they seem'd in sight
Which deck the baldric of the Heavens bright ;

They two, forth pacing to the river's side, 175
Received those two fair brides, their love's delight ;
    Which, at th' appointed tide,
    Each one did make his bride
Against their bridal day, which is not long : 179
Sweet Thames ! run softly, till I end my song.

E. Spenser.

54

THE HAPPY HEART

Art thou poor, yet hast thou golden slumbers ?
    O sweet content !
Art thou rich, yet is thy mind perplexed ?
    O punishment !
Dost thou laugh to see how fools are vexed 5
To add to golden numbers, golden numbers ?
O sweet content ! O sweet, O sweet content !
    Work apace, apace, apace, apace ;
    Honest labour bears a lovely face ;
Then hey nonny nonny, hey nonny nonny ! 10

Canst drink the waters of the crispéd spring ?
    O sweet content !
Swimm'st thou in wealth, yet sink'st in thine own
        tears ?
    O punishment !
Then he that patiently want's burden bears 15
No burden bears, but is a king, a king !
O sweet content ! O sweet, O sweet content !
    Work apace, apace, apace, apace ;
    Honest labour bears a lovely face ;
Then hey nonny nonny, hey nonny nonny ! 20

T. Dekker.

55

This Life, which seems so fair,
Is like a bubble blown up in the air
   By sporting children's breath,
    Who chase it everywhere   4
And strive who can most motion it bequeath.
And though it sometime seem of its own might,

   Like to an eye of gold, to be fix'd there,
And firm to hover in that empty height,
   That only is because it is so light.   9
  —But in that pomp it doth not long appear ;
For, when 'tis most admired, in a thought,
Because it erst was nought, it turns to nought.

W. DRUMMOND.

56

SOUL AND BODY

Poor Soul, the centre of my sinful earth,
  [Fool'd by] those rebel powers that thee array,
Why dost thou pine within, and suffer dearth,
  Painting thy outward walls so costly gay ?

Why so large cost, having so short a lease,   5
  Dost thou upon thy fading mansion spend ?
Shall worms, inheritors of this excess,
  Eat up thy charge ? is this thy body's end ?

Then, Soul, live thou upon thy servant's loss,
  And let that pine to aggravate thy store ;   10
Buy terms divine in selling hours of dross ;
  Within be fed, without be rich no more :—

So shalt thou feed on death, that feeds on men,
And death once dead, there's no more dying then.

W. SHAKESPEARE.

57

LIFE

The World's a bubble, and the Life of Man
  Less than a span :
In his conception wretched, from the womb
  So to the tomb ;
Curst from the cradle, and brought up to years
  With cares and fears.   6
Who then to frail mortality shall trust,
But limns the water, or but writes in dust.

Yet since with sorrow here we live opprest,
  What life is best ?   10
Courts are but only superficial schools
  To dandle fools :
The rural parts are turn'd into a den
  Of savage men :
And where's a city from all vice so free, 15
But may be term'd the worst of all the three ?

Domestic cares afflict the husband's bed,
  Or pains his head :
Those that live single, take it for a curse,
  Or do things worse :   20
Some would have children : those that have them
    moan
  Or wish them gone :
What is it, then, to have, or have no wife,
But single thraldom, or a double strife ?

Our own affections still at home to please 25
  Is a disease :
To cross the sea to any foreign soil,
  Perils and toil :
Wars with their noise affright us ; when they cease,
  We are worse in peace ;—   30
What then remains, but that we still should cry
Not to be born, or, being born, to die ?

          Lord Bacon.

58

THE LESSONS OF NATURE

Of this fair volume which we World do name
  If we the sheets and leaves could turn with care,
Of Him who it corrects, and did it frame,
  We clear might read the art and wisdom rare :

Find out His power which wildest powers doth
    tame, 5
  His providence extending everywhere,
  His justice which proud rebels doth not spare,
In every page, no period of the same.

But silly we, like foolish children, rest
  Well pleased with colour'd vellum, leaves of gold,
Fair dangling ribbands, leaving what is best, 11
  On the great Writer's sense ne'er taking hold ;

Or if by chance we stay our minds on aught,
It is some picture on the margin wrought.

                W. DRUMMOND.

59

Doth then the world go thus, doth all thus move ?
  Is this the justice which on Earth we find ?
  Is this that firm decree which all both bind ?
Are these your influences, Powers above ? 4

  Those souls which vice's moody mists most blind,
Blind Fortune, blindly, most their friend doth prove;
And they who thee, poor idol, Virtue ! love,
  Ply like a feather toss'd by storm and wind.

Ah ! if a Providence doth sway this all,
  Why should best minds groan under most dis-
    tress ? 10
Or why should pride humility make thrall,
  And injuries the innocent oppress ?

Heavens ! hinder, stop this fate ; or grant a time
When good may have, as well as bad, their prime.

                W. DRUMMOND.

60

THE WORLD'S WAY

Tired with all these, for restful death I cry—
  As, to behold desert a beggar born,
And needy nothing trimm'd in jollity,
  And purest faith unhappily forsworn,

And gilded honour shamefully misplaced,   5
  And maiden virtue rudely strumpeted,
And right perfection wrongfully disgraced,
  And strength by limping sway disabled,

And art made tongue-tied by authority,
  And folly, doctor-like, controlling skill,   10
And simple truth miscall'd simplicity,
  And captive Good attending captain Ill :—
—Tired with all these, from these would I be gone,
Save that, to die, I leave my Love alone.

W. Shakespeare.

61

SAINT JOHN BAPTIST

The last and greatest Herald of Heaven's King
  Girt with rough skins, hies to the deserts wild,
Among that savage brood the woods forth bring,
  Which he more harmless found than man, and
    mild.   4

His food was locusts, and what there doth spring,
  With honey that from virgin hives distill'd ;
Parch'd body, hollow eyes, some uncouth thing
  Made him appear, long since from earth exiled.

There burst he forth : ' All ye whose hopes rely
  On God, with me amidst these deserts mourn,
  Repent, repent, and from old errors turn !'   11
—Who listen'd to his voice, obey'd his cry ?

Only the echoes, which he made relent,
Rung from their flinty caves, Repent ! Repent !

W. Drummond.

THE GOLDEN TREASURY

BOOK SECOND

62

ODE ON THE
MORNING OF CHRIST'S NATIVITY

This is the month, and this the happy morn
   Wherein the Son of Heaven's Eternal King
Of wedded maid and virgin mother born,
    Our great redemption from above did bring ;
    For so the holy sages once did sing   5
That He our deadly forfeit should release,
And with His Father work us a perpetual peace.

That glorious Form, that Light unsufferable,
   And that far-beaming blaze of Majesty
Wherewith He wont at Heaven's high council-
    table   10
    To sit the midst of Trinal Unity,
    He laid aside ; and, here with us to be,
Forsook the courts of everlasting day,
And chose with us a darksome house of mortal clay.

Say, heavenly Muse, shall not thy sacred vein
   Afford a present to the Infant God ?   16
Hast thou no verse, no hymn, or solemn strain
    To welcome Him to this His new abode,
    Now while the heaven, by the sun's team un-
    trod,
Hath took no print of the approaching light,   20
And all the spangled host keep watch in squadrons
    bright ?

See how from far, upon the eastern road,
   The star-led wizards haste with odours sweet :
O run, prevent them with thy humble ode
    And lay it lowly at His blessed feet ;   25

Have thou the honour first thy Lord to greet,
And join thy voice unto the angel quire
From out His secret altar touch'd with hallow'd fire.

The Hymn

It was the winter wild
While the heaven-born Child   30
All meanly wrapt in the rude manger lies ;
    Nature in awe to Him
    Had doff'd her gaudy trim,
With her great Master so to sympathize :
    It was no season then for her   35
To wanton with the sun, her lusty paramour.

    Only with speeches fair
    She woos the gentle air
To hide her guilty front with innocent snow ;
    And on her naked shame,   40
    Pollute with sinful blame,
The saintly veil of maiden white to throw ;
Confounded, that her Maker's eyes
Should look so near upon her foul deformities.

    But He, her fears to cease,   45
    Sent down the meek-eyed Peace ;
She, crown'd with olive green, came softly sliding
    Down through the turning sphere,
    His ready harbinger,
With turtle wing the amorous clouds dividing ;
    And waving wide her myrtle wand,   51
She strikes a universal peace through sea and land.

    No war, or battle's sound
    Was heard the world around :
The idle spear and shield were high uphung ;   55
    The hookéd chariot stood
    Unstain'd with hostile blood ;
The trumpet spake not to the arméd throng ;
    And kings sat still with awful eye,
As if they surely knew their sovran Lord was by. 60

But peaceful was the night
 Wherein the Prince of Light
His reign of peace upon the earth began :
  The winds, with wonder whist,
  Smoothly the waters kist,   65
Whispering new joys to the mild ocêan—
 Who now hath quite forgot to rave,
While birds of calm sit brooding on the charméd
   wave.

  The stars, with deep amaze,
  Stand fix'd in steadfast gaze, 70
Bending one way their precious influence ;
  And will not take their flight
  For all the morning light,
Or Lucifer that often warn'd them thence ;
  But in their glimmering orbs did glow 75
Until their Lord Himself bespake, and bid them go.

  And though the shady gloom
  Had given day her room,
The sun himself withheld his wonted speed,
  And hid his head for shame, 80
  As his inferior flame
The new-enlighten'd world no more should need :
 He saw a greater Sun appear
Than his bright throne or burning axletree could
   bear.

  The shepherds on the lawn 85
  Or ere the point of dawn
Sate simply chatting in a rustic row ;
  Full little thought they than
  That the mighty Pan
Was kindly come to live with them below ; 90
 Perhaps their loves, or else their sheep
Was all that did their silly thoughts so busy keep.

  When such music sweet
  Their hearts and ears did greet
As never was by mortal finger strook— 95
  Divinely-warbled voice

Answering the stringéd noise,
As all their souls in blissful rapture took :
The air, such pleasure loth to lose,
With thousand echoes still prolongs each heavenly
close.   100

Nature that heard such sound
Beneath the hollow round
Of Cynthia's seat the airy region thrilling,
Now was almost won
To think her part was done,   105
And that her reign had here its last fulfilling ;
She knew such harmony alone
Could hold all heaven and earth in happier union.

At last surrounds their sight
A globe of circular light,   110
That with long beams the shamefaced night
array'd ;
The helméd Cherubim
And sworded Seraphim
Are seen in glittering ranks with wings display'd,
Harping in loud and solemn quire   115
With unexpressive notes; to Heaven's new-born
Heir.

Such music (as 'tis said)
Before was never made
But when of old the sons of morning sung,
While the Creator great   120
His constellations set
And the well-balanced world on hinges hung ;
And cast the dark foundations deep,
And bid the weltering waves their oozy channel
keep.

Ring out, ye crystal spheres !   125
Once bless our human ears,
If ye have power to touch our senses so ;
And let your silver chime
Move in melodious time ;
And let the bass of heaven's deep organ blow ,

And with your ninefold harmony 131
Make up full consort to the angelic symphony.

For if such holy song,
Enwrap our fancy long,
Time will run back, and fetch the age of gold ;
And speckled vanity 136
Will sicken soon and die,
And leprous sin will melt from earthly mould ;
And Hell itself will pass away,
And leave her dolorous mansions to the peering day.

Yea, Truth and Justice then 141
Will down return to men,
Orb'd in a rainbow ; and, like glories wearing,
Mercy will sit between
Throned in celestial sheen, 145
With radiant feet the tissued clouds down
steering ;
And Heaven, as at some festival,
Will open wide the gates of her high palace hall.

But wisest Fate says No ;
This must not yet be so ; 150
The Babe yet lies in smiling infancy
That on the bitter cross
Must redeem our loss ;
So both Himself and us to glorify :
Yet first, to those ychain'd in sleep 155
The wakeful trump of doom must thunder through
the deep,

With such a horrid clang
As on mount Sinai rang
While the red fire and smouldering clouds out-
brake :
The aged Earth aghast 160
With terror of that blast
Shall from the surface to the centre shake,
When, at the world's last sessión,
The dreadful Judge in middle air shall spread His
throne.

And then at last our bliss   165
   Full and perfect is,
But now begins ; for from this happy day
   The old Dragon under ground,
   In straiter limits bound,
Not half so far casts his usurpéd sway ;   170
   And, wroth to see his kingdom fail,
Swinges the scaly horror of his folded tail.

   The oracles are dumb ;
   No voice or hideous hum
Runs through the archéd roof in words deceiving :
   Apollo from his shrine   176
   Can no more divine,
With hollow shriek the steep of Delphos leaving :
   No nightly trance or breathéd spell
Inspires the pale-eyed priest from the prophetic cell.

   The lonely mountains o'er   181
   And the resounding shore
A voice of weeping heard, and loud lament ;
   From haunted spring and dale
   Edged with poplar pale   185
The parting Genius is with sighing sent ;
   With flower-inwoven tresses torn
The nymphs in twilight shade of tangled thickets
     mourn.

   In consecrated earth
   And on the holy hearth   190
The Lars and Lemures moan with midnight
     plaint ;
   In urns, and altars round
   A drear and dying sound
Affrights the Flamens at their service quaint ;
   And the chill marble seems to sweat,   195
While each peculiar Power forgoes his wonted seat.

   Peor and Baalim
   Forsake their temples dim,
With that twice-batter'd god of Palestine ;
   And mooned Ashtaroth   200
   Heaven's queen and mother both,

Now sits not girt with tapers' holy shine ;
 The Lybic Hammon shrinks his horn,
In vain the Tyrian maids their wounded Thammuz
  mourn.

  And sullen Moloch, fled,   205
   Hath left in shadows dread
His burning idol all of blackest hue ;
  In vain with cymbals' ring
  They call the grisly king,
In dismal dance about the furnace blue ; 210
 The brutish gods of Nile as fast,
Isis, and Orus, and the dog Anubis, haste.

  Nor is Osiris seen
   In Memphian grove, or green,
Trampling the unshower'd grass with lowings
  loud :   215
  Nor can he be at rest
  Within his sacred chest ;
Nought but profoundest hell can be his shroud ;
 In vain with timbrell'd anthems dark
The sable-stoléd sorcerers bear his worshipt ark.

  He feels from Juda's land   221
   The dreaded infant's hand ;
The rays of Bethlehem blind his dusky eyn ;
  Nor all the gods beside
  Longer dare abide,   225
Not Typhon huge ending in snaky twine :
 Our Babe, to show his Godhead true,
Can in His swaddling bands control the damnéd
  crew.

  So, when the sun in bed
   Curtain'd with cloudy red 230
Pillows his chin upon an orient wave,
  The flocking shadows pale
  Troop to the infernal jail,
Each fetter'd ghost slips to his several grave ;
  And the yellow-skirted fays 235
Fly after the night-steeds, leaving their moon-loved
  maze.

But see, the Virgin blest
Hath laid her Babe to rest ;
Time is, our tedious song should here have
    ending :
    Heaven's youngest-teeméd star   240
    Hath fix'd her polish'd car,
Her sleeping Lord with hand-maid lamp attend-
    ing :
    And all about the courtly stable
Bright-harness'd angels sit in order serviceable.

J. MILTON.

63

SONG FOR SAINT CECILIA'S DAY, 1687

From Harmony, from heavenly Harmony
    This universal frame began :
    When Nature underneath a heap
        Of jarring atoms lay
And could not heave her head,   5
The tuneful voice was heard from high
        Arise, ye more than dead !
Then cold, and hot, and moist, and dry
In order to their stations leap,
    And Music's power obey.   10
From harmony, from heavenly harmony
    This universal frame began :
        From harmony to harmony
Through all the compass of the notes it ran,
The diapason closing full in Man.   15

What passion cannot Music raise and quell ?
    When Jubal struck the chorded shell
His listening brethren stood around,
    And, wondering, on their faces fell
To worship that celestial sound.   20
Less than a god they thought there could not
    dwell
        Within the hollow of that shell
        That spoke so sweetly and so well.
What passion cannot Music raise and quell ?

The trumpet's loud clangor   25
  Excites us to arms,
With shrill notes of anger
  And mortal alarms.
The double double double beat
  Of the thundering drum   30
Cries ' Hark ! the foes come ;
Charge, charge, 'tis too late to retreat !'

The soft complaining flute
  In dying notes discovers
The woes of hopeless lovers,   35
Whose dirge is whisper'd by the warbling lute.

Sharp violins proclaim
Their jealous pangs and desperation,
Fury, frantic indignation,
Depth of pains, and height of passion   40
  For the fair disdainful dame.

But oh ! what art can teach,
What human voice can reach
  The sacred organ's praise ?
Notes inspiring holy love,   45
  Notes that wing their heavenly ways
To mend the choirs above.

Orpheus could lead the savage race,
And trees unrooted left their place
  Sequacious of the lyre :   50
But bright Cecilia raised the wonder higher :
When to her Organ vocal breath was given,
An Angel heard, and straight appear'd—
  Mistaking Earth for Heaven !

Grand Chorus

As from the power of sacred lays   55
  The spheres began to move,
And sung the great Creator's praise
  To all the blest above ;

So when the last and dreadful hour
This crumbling pageant shall devour   60
The trumpet shall be heard on high,
The dead shall live, the living die,
And Music shall untune the sky.
J. DRYDEN.

64

ON THE LATE MASSACRE IN PIEDMONT

Avenge, O Lord! Thy slaughter'd Saints, whose bones
  Lie scatter'd on the Alpine mountains cold;
  Even them who kept Thy truth so pure of old,
When all our fathers worshipt stocks and stones,

Forget not: in Thy book record their groans   5
  Who were Thy sheep, and in their ancient fold
  Slain by the bloody Piemontese, that roll'd
Mother with infant down the rocks. Their moans

The vales redoubled to the hills, and they   9
  To Heaven. Their martyr'd blood and ashes sow
  O'er all the Italian fields, where still doth sway

The triple tyrant: that from these may grow
A hundred-fold, who, having learnt Thy way,
  Early may fly the Babylonian woe.
J. MILTON.

65

HORATIAN ODE UPON CROMWELL'S RETURN FROM IRELAND

The forward youth that would appear,
Must now forsake his Muses dear,
  Nor in the shadows sing
  His numbers languishing.

'Tis time to leave the books in dust,   5
And oil th' unuséd armour's rust,
  Removing from the wall
  The corslet of the hall.

So restless Cromwell could not cease
In the inglorious arts of peace,   10
    But through adventurous war
    Urgéd his active star :

And like the three-fork'd lightning, first
Breaking the clouds where it was nurst,
    Did thorough his own side   15
    His fiery way divide :

(For 'tis all one to courage high
The emulous, or enemy ;
    And with such, to enclose
    Is more than to oppose ;)   20

Then burning through the air he went
And palaces and temples rent ;
    And Caesar's head at last
    Did through his laurels blast.

'Tis madness to resist or blame   25
The face of angry heaven's flame ;
    And if we would speak true,
    Much to the man is due

Who, from his private gardens, where
He lived reservéd and austere   30
    (As if his highest plot
    To plant the bergamot),

Could by industrious valour climb
To ruin the great work of Time,
    And cast the Kingdoms old   35
    Into another mould ;

Though Justice against Fate complain,
And plead the ancient Rights in vain—
    But those do hold or break
    As men are strong or weak.   40

Nature, that hateth emptiness,
Allows of penetration less,
    And therefore must make room
    Where greater spirits come.

What field of all the Civil War   45
Where his were not the deepest scar ?
    And Hampton shows what part
    He had of wiser art ;

Where, twining subtle fears with hope,
He wove a net of such a scope   50
    That Charles himself might chase
    To Carisbrook's narrow case ;

That thence the Royal actor borne
The tragic scaffold might adorn :
    While round the arméd bands   55
    Did clap their bloody hands ;

He nothing common did or mean
Upon that memorable scene,
    But with his keener eye
    The axe's edge did try ;   60

Nor call'd the Gods, with vulgar spite,
To vindicate his helpless right ;
    But bow'd his comely head
    Down, as upon a bed.

—This was that memorable hour   65
Which first assured the forcéd power
    So when they did design
    The Capitol's first line,

A Bleeding Head, where they begun,
Did fright the architects to run ;   70
    And yet in that the State
    Foresaw its happy fate !

And now the Irish are ashamed
To see themselves in one year tamed :
    So much one man can do   75
    That does both act and know.

They can affirm his praises best,
And have, though overcome, confest
    How good he is, how just
    And fit for highest trust ;   80

Nor yet grown stiffer with command,
But still in the Republic's hand—
    How fit he is to sway
    That can so well obey !—

He to the Commons' feet presents   85
A Kingdom for his first year's rents,
    And (what he may) forbears
    His fame, to make it theirs :

And has his sword and spoils ungirt
To lay them at the Public's skirt.   90
    So when the falcon high
    Falls heavy from the sky,

She, having kill'd, no more does search
But on the next green bough to perch,
    Where, when he first does lure,   95
    The falconer has her sure.

—What may not then our Isle presume
While victory his crest does plume ?
    What may not others fear
    If thus he crowns each year ?   100

As Caesar he, ere long, to Gaul,
To Italy an Hannibal,
    And to all states not free
    Shall climacteric be.

The Pict no shelter now shall find   105
Within his parti-colour'd mind,
    But from this valour sad,
    Shrink underneath the plaid—

Happy, if in the tufted brake
The English hunter him mistake,   110
    Nor lay his hounds in near
    The Caledonian deer.

But thou, the War's and Fortune's son,
March indefatigably on ;
    And for the last effect   115
    Still keep the sword erect :

To sport with Amaryllis in the shade,
Or with the tangles of Neaera's hair ?   69
Fame is the spur that the clear spirit doth raise
(That last infirmity of noble mind)
To scorn delights, and live laborious days ;
But the fair guerdon when we hope to find,
And think to burst out into sudden blaze,   74
Comes the blind Fury with the abhorréd shears
And slits the thin-spun life. ' But not the praise '
Phoebus replied, and touch'd my trembling ears ;
' Fame is no plant that grows on mortal soil,
Nor in the glistering foil   79
Set off to the world, nor in broad rumour lies :
But lives and spreads aloft by those pure eyes
And perfect witness of all-judging Jove ;
As he pronounces lastly on each deed,
Of so much fame in heaven expect thy meed.'   84

  O fountain Arethuse, and thou honour'd flood
Smooth-sliding Mincius, crown'd with vocal reeds,
That strain I heard was of a higher mood :
But now my oat proceeds,
And listens to the herald of the sea
That came in Neptune's plea ;   90
He ask'd the waves, and ask'd the felon winds,
What hard mishap hath doom'd this gentle swain ?
And question'd every gust of rugged wings
That blows from off each beakéd promontory :
They knew not of his story ;   95
And sage Hippotades their answer brings,
That not a blast was from his dungeon stray'd ;
The air was calm, and on the level brine
Sleek Panope with all her sisters play'd.
It was that fatal and perfidious bark   100
Built in the eclipse, and rigg'd with curses dark,
That sunk so low that sacred head of thine.

  Next Camus, reverend sire, went footing slow,
His mantle hairy, and his bonnet sedge,
Inwrought with figures dim, and on the edge   105
Like to that sanguine flower inscribed with woe :

'Ah! who hath reft,' quoth he, 'my dearest
    pledge?'
Last came, and last did go
The pilot of the Galilean lake;
Two massy keys he bore of metals twain   110
(The golden opes, the iron shuts amain);
He shook his mitred locks, and stern bespake:
'How well could I have spared for thee, young
    swain,
Enow of such as for their bellies' sake
Creep and intrude and climb into the fold!   115
Of other care they little reckoning make
Than how to scramble at the shearers' feast,
And shove away the worthy bidden guest.
Blind mouths! that scarce themselves know how
    to hold
A sheep-hook, or have learn'd aught else the least
That to the faithful herdman's art belongs!   121
What recks it them? What need they? They
    are sped;
And when they list, their lean and flashy songs
Grate on their scrannel pipes of wretched straw;
The hungry sheep look up, and are not fed,   125
But swoln with wind and the rank mist they draw
Rot inwardly, and foul contagion spread:
Besides what the grim wolf with privy paw
Daily devours apace, and nothing said:
—But that two-handed engine at the door   130
Stands ready to smite once, and smite no more.'

    Return, Alpheus, the dread voice is past
That shrunk thy streams; return, Sicilian Muse,
And call the vales, and bid them hither cast
Their bells and flowerets of a thousand hues.   135
Ye valleys low, where the mild whispers use
Of shades, and wanton winds, and gushing brooks,
On whose fresh lap the swart star sparely looks,
Throw hither all your quaint enamell'd eyes   139
That on the green turf suck the honey'd showers
And purple all the ground with vernal flowers.

Bring the rathe primrose that forsaken dies;
The tufted crow-toe, and pale jessamine,
The white pink, and the pansy freak'd with jet,
The glowing violet, 145
The musk-rose, and the well-attired woodbine,
With cowslips wan that hang the pensive head,
And every flower that sad embroidery wears:
Bid amarantus all his beauty shed,
And daffadillies fill their cups with tears 150
To strew the laureat hearse where Lycid lies.
For, so to interpose a little ease,
Let our frail thoughts dally with false surmise;
Ay me! whilst thee the shores and sounding seas
Wash far away,—where'er thy bones are hurl'd,
Whether beyond the stormy Hebrides 156
Where thou perhaps, under the whelming tide,
Visitest the bottom of the monstrous world;
Or whether thou, to our moist vows denied,
Sleep'st by the fable of Bellerus old, 160
Where the great Vision of the guarded mount
Looks toward Namancos and Bayona's hold,
—Look homeward, Angel, now, and melt with
    ruth:
—And, O ye dolphins, waft the hapless youth!

Weep no more, woeful shepherds, weep no
    more, 165
For Lycidas, your sorrow, is not dead,
Sunk though he be beneath the watery floor;
So sinks the day-star in the ocean-bed,
And yet anon repairs his drooping head
And tricks his beams, and with new-spangled ore
Flames in the forehead of the morning sky: 171
So Lycidas sunk low, but mounted high
Through the dear might of Him that walk'd the
    waves;
Where, other groves and other streams along,
With nectar pure his oozy locks he laves, 175
And hears the unexpressive nuptial song
In the blest kingdoms meek of joy and love.

There entertain him all the saints above
In solemn troops, and sweet societies,
That sing, and singing in their glory move,   180
And wipe the tears for ever from his eyes.
Now, Lycidas, the shepherds weep no more ;
Henceforth thou art the Genius of the shore
In thy large recompense, and shalt be good
To all that wander in that perilous flood.   185

Thus sang the uncouth swain to the oaks and rills,
While the still morn went out with sandals grey ;
He touch'd the tender stops of various quills,
With eager thought warbling his Doric lay :
And now the sun had stretch'd out all the hills,
And now was dropt into the western bay :   191
At last he rose, and twitch'd his mantle blue :
To-morrow to fresh woods, and pastures new.

J. MILTON.

67

ON THE TOMBS IN WESTMINSTER ABBEY

Mortality, behold and fear,
What a change of flesh is here !
Think how many royal bones
Sleep within these heaps of stones ;
Here they lie, had realms and lands,   5
Who now want strength to stir their hands,
Where from their pulpits seal'd with dust
They preach, ' In greatness is no trust.'
Here's an acre sown indeed
With the richest royallest seed   10
That the earth did e'er suck in
Since the first man died for sin :
Here the bones of birth have cried
' Though gods they were, as men they died ! '
Here are sands, ignoble things,   15
Dropt from the ruin'd sides of kings :
Here's a world of pomp and state
Buried in dust, once dead by fate.

F. BEAUMONT.

68

THE LAST CONQUEROR

Victorious men of earth, no more
  Proclaim how wide your empires are ;
Though you bind-in every shore,
    And your triumphs reach as far
      As night or day,   5
  Yet you, proud monarchs, must obey
And mingle with forgotten ashes, when
Death calls ye to the crowd of common men.

Devouring Famine, Plague, and War,
  Each able to undo mankind,   10
Death's servile emissaries are ;
    Nor to these alone confined,
      He hath at will
  More quaint and subtle ways to kill ;
A smile or kiss, as he will use the art,   15
Shall have the cunning skill to break a heart.
                    J. SHIRLEY.

69

DEATH THE LEVELLER

The glories of our blood and state
    Are shadows, not substantial things ;
There is no armour against fate ;
    Death lays his icy hand on kings :
      Sceptre and Crown   5
      Must tumble down,
And in the dust be equal made
With the poor crooked scythe and spade.

Some men with swords may reap the field,   9
    And plant fresh laurels where they kill :
But their strong nerves at last must yield ;
    They tame but one another still :

Early or late
They stoop to fate,
And must give up their murmuring breath   15
When they, pale captives, creep to death.

The garlands wither on your brow ;
    Then boast no more your mighty deeds ;
Upon Death's purple altar now
    See where the victor-victim bleeds :   20
        Your heads must come
        To the cold tomb ;
Only the actions of the just
Smell sweet, and blossom in their dust.

J. SHIRLEY.

70

WHEN THE ASSAULT WAS INTENDED
TO THE CITY

Captain, or Colonel, or Knight in arms,
    Whose chance on these defenceless doors may
        seize,
If deed of honour did thee ever please,
Guard them, and him within protect from harms.

He can requite thee ; for he knows the charms
    That call fame on such gentle acts as these,   6
    And he can spread thy name o'er lands and seas,
Whatever clime the sun's bright circle warms.

Lift not thy spear against the Muses' bower :
    The great Emathian conqueror bid spare   10
The house of Pindarus, when temple and tower

Went to the ground : and the repeated air
Of sad Electra's poet had the power
    To save the Athenian walls from ruin bare.

J. MILTON

71

ON HIS BLINDNESS

When I consider how my light is spent
　　Ere half my days, in this dark world and wide,
　　And that one talent which is death to hide
Lodged with me useless, though my soul more bent

To serve therewith my Maker, and present　　5
　　My true account, lest He returning chide,—
　　Doth God exact day-labour, light denied?
I fondly ask:—But Patience, to prevent

That murmur, soon replies; God doth not need
　　Either man's work, or His own gifts: who best
　　Bear His mild yoke, they serve Him best: His
　　　　state　　11

Is kingly; thousands at His bidding speed
　　And post o'er land and ocean without rest:—
　　They also serve who only stand and wait.

　　　　　　　　　　　　　J. MILTON.

72

CHARACTER OF A HAPPY LIFE

How happy is he born or taught
　　That serveth not another's will;
Whose armour is his honest thought,
　　And silly truth his highest skill!

Whose passions not his masters are,　　5
　　Whose soul is still prepared for death;
Untied unto the world with care
　　Of princely love or vulgar breath;

Who hath his life from rumours freed,
　　Whose conscience is his strong retreat　　10
Whose state can neither flatterers feed,
　　Nor ruin make accusers great;

Who envieth none whom chance doth raise
  Or vice ; who never understood   14
How deepest wounds are given with praise ;
  Nor rules of state, but rules of good :

Who God doth late and early pray
  More of his grace than gifts to lend ;
Who entertains the harmless day
  With a well-chosen book or friend ;   20

—This man is free from servile bands
  Of hope to rise, or fear to fall ;
Lord of himself, though not of lands ;
  And having nothing, he hath all.

SIR H. WOTTON.

73

THE NOBLE NATURE

It is not growing like a tree
  In bulk, doth make Man better be ;
Or standing long an oak, three hundred year,
To fall a log at last, dry, bald, and sere :
    A lily of a day   5
    Is fairer far in May,
  Although it fall and die that night ;
  It was the plant and flower of Light.
In small proportions we just beauties see ;
And in short measures life may perfect be.   10

B. JONSON.

74

THE GIFTS OF GOD

When God at first made Man,
Having a glass of blessings standing by ;
Let us (said He) pour on him all we can :
Let the world's riches, which dispersèd lie,
    Contract into a span.   5

So strength first made a way ;
Then beauty flow'd, then wisdom, honour, pleasure :
When almost all was out, God made a stay,
Perceiving that alone, of all His treasure,
     Rest in the bottom lay.   10

For if I should (said He)
Bestow this jewel also on my creature,
He would adore my gifts instead of me,
And rest in Nature, not the God of Nature :
     So both should losers be.   15

Yet let him keep the rest,
But keep them with repining restlessness :
Let him be rich and weary, that at least,
If goodness lead him not, yet weariness
     May toss him to my breast.   20

              G. HERBERT.

75

THE RETREAT

Happy those early days, when I
Shined in my Angel-infancy !
Before I understood this place
Appointed for my second race,
Or taught my soul to fancy aught   5
But a white, celestial thought ;
When yet I had not walk'd above
A mile or two from my first Love,
And looking back, at that short space
Could see a glimpse of His bright face ;   10
When on some gilded cloud or flower
My gazing soul would dwell an hour,
And in those weaker glories spy
Some shadows of eternity ;
Before I taught my tongue to wound   15
My conscience with a sinful sound,
Or had the black art to dispense
A several sin to every sense,

But felt through all this fleshly dress
Bright shoots of everlastingness.   20

O how I long to travel back,
And tread again that ancient track !
That I might once more reach that plain,
Where first I left my glorious train ;
From whence th' enlighten'd spirit sees   25
That shady City of Palm trees !
But ah ! my soul with too much stay
Is drunk, and staggers in the way :—
Some men a forward motion love,
But I by backward steps would move ;   30
And when this dust falls to the urn,
In that state I came, return.

                  H. VAUGHAN.

76

TO MR. LAWRENCE

Lawrence, of virtuous father virtuous son,
  Now that the fields are dank and ways are mire,
  Where shall we sometimes meet, and by the fire
Help waste a sullen day, what may be won

From the hard season gaining ? Time will run
  On smoother, till Favonius re-inspire   6
  The frozen earth, and clothe in fresh attire
The lily and rose, that neither sow'd nor spun.

What neat repast shall feast us, light and choice,
  Of Attic taste, with wine, whence we may rise
To hear the lute well touch'd, or artful voice   11

    Warble immortal notes and Tuscan air ?
    He who of those delights can judge, and spare
To interpose them oft, is not unwise.

                  J. MILTON.

77

TO CYRIACK SKINNER

Cyriack, whose grandsire, on the royal bench
    Of British Themis, with no mean applause
    Pronounced, and in his volumes taught, our laws,
Which others at their bar so often wrench ;   4

To-day deep thoughts resolve with me to drench
    In mirth, that after no repenting draws ;
    Let Euclid rest, and Archimedes pause,
And what the Swede intend, and what the French.

To measure life learn thou betimes, and know   9
    Toward solid good what leads the nearest way ;
    For other things mild Heaven a time ordains,

And disapproves that care, though wise in show,
    That with superfluous burden loads the day,
    And, when God sends a cheerful hour, refrains.

                    J. MILTON.

78

HYMN TO DIANA

Queen and Huntress, chaste and fair,
    Now the sun is laid to sleep,
Seated in thy silver chair
    State in wonted manner keep :
        Hesperus entreats thy light,   5
        Goddess excellently bright.

Earth, let not thy envious shade
    Dare itself to interpose ;
Cynthia's shining orb was made
    Heaven to clear when day did close :   10
        Bless us then with wishéd sight,
        Goddess excellently bright.

Lay thy bow of pearl apart
    And thy crystal-shining quiver ;
Give unto the flying hart   15
        Space to breathe, how short soever :
            Thou that mak'st a day of night,
            Goddess excellently bright !
                                B. JONSON.

79

WISHES FOR THE SUPPOSED MISTRESS

Whoe'er she be,
    That not impossible She
That shall command my heart and me ;

    Where'er she lie,
    Lock'd up from mortal eye   5
In shady leaves of destiny :

    Till that ripe birth
    Of studied Fate stand forth,
And teach her fair steps tread our earth ;

    Till that divine   10
    Idea take a shrine
Of crystal flesh, through which to shine :

    —Meet you her, my Wishes,
    Bespeak her to my blisses,
And be ye call'd, my absent kisses.   15

    I wish her beauty
    That owes not all its duty
To gaudy tire, or glist'ring shoe-tie :

    Something more than
    Taffata or tissue can,   20
Or rampant feather, or rich fan.

    A face that 's best
    By its own beauty drest,
And can alone commend the rest :